One in the Faith

One in the Faith

HARRY HUXHOLD

C.S.S. Publishing Co., Inc.
Lima, Ohio

ONE IN THE FAITH

Copyright © 1988 by
The C.S.S. Publishing Company, Inc.
Lima, Ohio

All rights reserved. No part of this publication may be reproduced, stored in a retrieval system, or transmitted in any form or by any means, electronic, mechanical, photocopying, recording, or otherwise, without the prior permission of the publisher. Inquiries should be addressed to: The C.S.S. Publishing Company, Inc., 628 South Main Street, Lima, Ohio 45804.

Library of Congress Cataloging-in-Publication Data

Huxhold, Harry N.
  One in the faith.

  1. Church year sermons. 2. Sermons, American. I. Title.
BV4253.H87 1988   252'.6   88-4277
ISBN 1-55673-060-8

Table of Contents

Introduction		8
A Note concerning Lectionaries and Calenders		9
The Day of Pentecost	*One in Language* *Genesis 11:1-9*	11
The Holy Trinity	*One in Three* *Proverbs 8:22-31*	18
Proper 4[1] **Pentecost 2**[2] **Corpus Christi** [3]	*One in Prayer* *1 Kings 8:22-23, 41-43*	26
Proper 5 **Pentecost 3** **Ordinary Time 10**	*One Word of Truth* *1 Kings 17:17-24*	33
Proper 6 **Pentecost 4** **Ordinary Time 11**	*One Lonely Prophet* *1 Kings 19:1-8*	41
Proper 7 **Pentecost 5** **Ordinary Time 12**	*One Still Small Voice* *1 Kings 19:9-14*	49
Proper 8 **Pentecost 6** **Ordinary Time 13**	*One Call to Follow* *1 Kings 19:15-21*	56
Proper 9 **Pentecost 7** **Ordinary Time 14**	*One Word of Judgment* *1 Kings 21:1-3, 17-21*	64
Proper 10 **Pentecost 8** **Ordinary Time 15**	*One Vision of Glory* *2 Kings 2:1, 6-14*	72

[1] Common Lectionary
[2] Lutheran Lectionary
[3] Roman Catholic Lectionary

To
The People of God
at
Our Redeemer Lutheran Church
Indianapolis, Indiana

Introduction

Preaching the texts from the Hebrew Scriptures was a particular joy for Martin Luther. For him this was the story of the church. If one wanted to know how God treats the people of God, the church, one had to look to the Hebrew Scriptures.

That is richly illustrated in these lessons for the first third of the Pentecost cycle, in which the prophetic voice is sounded faithfully. At the same time we learn how the prophets themselves had to hear the Gospel for their strengthening.

Story is encouraged as an effective homiletical art form in our time. These texts lend themselves to the preachers as excellent opportunities for them to test their skills as Gospel story tellers.

Harry N. Huxhold

A Note Concerning Lectionaries and Calendars

The following index will aid the user of this book in matching the right Sunday with the appropriate text during the second half of the church year. Days listed here include only those appropriate to the contents of this book:

Fixed-date Lectionaries

Common	Roman Catholic	Lutheran Lectionary
Proper 4 *May 29 — June 4*	Corpus Christi	Pentecost 2
Proper 5 *June 5-11*	Ordinary Time 10	Pentecost 3
Proper 6 *June 12-18*	Ordinary Time 11	Pentecost 4
Proper 7 *June 19-25*	Ordinary Time 12	Pentecost 5
Proper 8 *June 26 — July 2*	Ordinary Time 13	Pentecost 6
Proper 9 *July 3-9*	Ordinary Time 14	Pentecost 7
Proper 10 *July 10-16*	Ordinary Time 15	Pentecost 8

Now the whole earth had one language and few words. And as men migrated from the east, they found a plain in the land of Shinar and settled there. And they said to one another, "Come, let us make bricks, and burn them thoroughly." And they had bricks for stone, and bitumen for mortar. Then they said, "Come, let us build ourselves a city, and a tower with its top in the heavens, and let us make a name for ourselves, lest we be scattered abroad upon the face of the whole earth." And the Lord came down to see the city and the tower, which the sons of men had built. And the Lord said, "Behold, they are one people, and they have all one language; and this is only the beginning of what they will do; and nothing that they propose to do will now be impossible for them. Come, let us go down, and there confuse their language, that they may not understand one another's speech." So the Lord scattered them abroad from there over the face of all the earth, and they left off building the city. Therefore its name was called Babel, because there the Lord confused the language of all the earth; and from there the Lord scattered them abroad over the face of all the earth.

Genesis 11:1-9

Genesis 11:1-9	The Day of Pentecost

One in Language

Our celebration of Pentecost is the recognition of the work of the Holy Spirit. On the first Pentecost the company of the faithful followers of Jesus were witnesses to the ability of God's Spirit to create faith in the hearts of people. This is a mighty act of God no less miraculous or dramatic than any other act of God. In doing this work God enables people to do the impossible. Scripture plainly teaches the reality that no one can say that Jesus is Lord but by the Holy Spirit. (1 Corinthians 12:3) When we hear someone confess the Lord Jesus Christ, God continues the work of Pentecost and we are witnesses to a mighty act of God.

Our hearts can fill with joy as we celebrate this day and acknowledge that the Holy Spirit is present among us. We take the occasion to make it clear that the Spirit is present among us. That is the purpose of the account of the first Christian Pentecost in the Book of Acts, which is Luke's record of how the Holy Spirit continued to work in the earth after the ascension of our Lord. Out of many languages the Spirit made clear one Word, and filled language with God's power.

The Marvel of Language

Many people had come to Jerusalem to celebrate the Jewish Feast of Pentecost. Because Jews had been dispersed throughout the world, these people came from many lands and spoke different languages. It is doubtful that many of them spoke Hebrew. Most of them probably knew the language that was popular throughout the world of that day, the *Koine*, that is, common Greek. However, before we speak of the many languages, it is important to reflect on the gift of language itself. The root word for language is from the Latin *lingua*, tongue. It is a blessing that we can use the tongue to make the distinguishable sounds we call language. Our ability to do so is plainly a gift from our Creator God.

When we try to explain the gift of language, we are forced to concede that it is not only a marvel but a mystery. Many theories have been advanced to explain the origin of language, but no matter how elaborate the explanation, we have to bow before the fact that language is a special gift. By faith we discern that it is a special gift from God by which we are able to communicate with regard to our emotions, our needs, our worship, and our vocations. That we are so endowed enables us to engage ourselves in the business of living in a way that lesser creatures within the creation are not able.

Why So Many Languages?

However, why are there many languages and dialects in the earth? Differences in language dialects are definite barriers and hindrances in communications between people who want to live together. Scholars who study language are not too clear on this point. They can find some similarities in the families of languages, but there are languages which show no relationships whatsoever. In the ancient account of the Tower of Babel people abandoned their project of building a tower that would reach into the heavens. They gave up this effort because God confused their language and they could not understand one another. What happened? We do not have the details, and we do not know how the confusion actually manifested itself. However, the story is clear on one point. The confusion of language was a judgment on people for their pride.

It is pride that alienates and separates people from one another. It is pride that erects barriers between people and makes them unable to communicate. One can sense this as one travels in foreign countries where people may use and know the language of the tourists but refuse to engage in conversation or offer help by hiding behind the barrier of their language. The Hebrew Scriptures are consistent in making this observation about differences in language. People were recognized as being essentially different when they spoke another language. They were strange and alien to one another. And do we not have to ask: are not the differences cultivated and protected by people because in their pride they want to be different from one another?

The Search for Oneness

It is important that we then strive to overcome the pride that divides people! We must look for those means by which we can get people to reason together, to speak together, and to dialog with one another. We can begin by exploring the similarities of language. One way of teaching a new language is to start the beginner out with the words that one already knows from another language. There have been attempts at creating a world language. We know how missionaries have worked with pidgin English. There have been efforts to create a language for diplomatic purposes. The great spread of English speaking people through the growth of the British Empire in the last century, and the world wars of this century had so popularized English that it almost became a world language.

People who live in the proximity of other people speaking different languages of necessity often develop good language facility. One can take a tour in Europe to hear a guide give tour explanations in up to seven different languages. However, in spite of the hopeful signs of speaking as one people, we still see people unable to communicate even when they speak the same tongue. Pride still keeps them apart.

The Root of the Problem

We are dreadfully conscious of the problem of communication in our time. Some people hold that the older generation is totally incapable of communicating with the young. Others believe that we cannot have meaningful dialog between the races. You can add as many different kinds of groups as you want — churches, labor and management, and the like. Again the problem is always the same. It is not simply the language that is the problem. It is pride. The Scriptures once more have a realistic view of the problem. The Hebrew Scriptures pictured the tongue as the instrument of the heart. Our Lord also made it clear that it was not what came out of a person's mouth that defiled one, but what came out of the heart.

It is not surprising then that in order to rescue people from the perils of their own language, God alone would have to speak to them. This is what God chose to do through Jesus Christ, our Lord. Jesus is called the Word of God. Jesus is the incarnate Word of God, the Word of God become flesh. What in gracious love God revealed under promises and the offices of prophets, priests, and kings, God now revealed more fully in the Son. The lessons God taught in great and mighty acts, through the spokesmen, the prophets; the servants, the priests; and the rulers, the kings; were not always clear to the people. In Jesus God now spoke as intelligibly and dramatically as possible. In Jesus God gave the clearest and best expression to people possible.

What was it that God spoke to us through the Son? God spoke a language of judgment and of love. In Jesus God demonstrated divine wrath as God permitted God's Son to be the victim of the hatred of people. Those who put Jesus to death heard God's language — God's words and message. But they would not believe. It was not because they did not understand. It was because they would not trust God's Word. Therefore Jesus was put to death for the sin of people, on account of their sin, and as a result of their sin.

However, the incarnate Word would not be silenced. God raised the Son, saying most clearly to the world that in this Son there was life and hope for all of the world. Pentecost was the day when the disciples by the gift of God's Spirit awoke to the implications of all that this meant. The disciples broke into the streets to tell all Jerusalem what the consequences were of the death of Jesus Christ. All Jerusalem could now know that the city that had put Jesus to death could now be brought to life through this same Christ. And those who formerly could not understand could now discern in the languages of the disciples the Word of God. "We hear them telling in our own tongues the mighty works of God." What was important was not that they heard their own language, but that with the heart they could hear and believe the mighty works of God.

We Can Speak His Language

That is the most important sign, miracle, wonder, marvel — call it what you will — of all. By the gift of God's Spirit we can hear and know the works of God and believe them because of our Lord Jesus Christ. May we never forget that! Through all of the ranting, shouting, polarizing, and debating that goes on in life, may we always hear clearly and intelligibly the love language which our God speaks to us through our Lord Jesus Christ! In the world there are many factors causing disharmony and disunity among people. Even within the church we discover people who believe that they should cause Christians to be at odds with one another. Whenever that happens, we need to ask, "Can we hear in our own tongues the mighty works of God?"

If we cannot hear the clear, plain, and intelligible witness to the fact that God has redeemed us through the Lord Jesus Christ, then we have every right to hold those suspect who pretend to speak in the name of our God. We are bombarded on all sides by all kinds of voices, languages, philosophies, and ideas. We must engage ourselves in worship and the study of

God's Word so that we are equipped always to hear and recognize the Gospel of our Lord Jesus Christ.

Babel Reversed

What the Pentecost story means to us then is that God has reversed the disorder of Babel. The judgment that had separated people because of their pride has now been overcome by the singular language of love which God has spoken to us in Jesus Christ. Strangely enough, it was within one generation that the church was thrown into disorder at Corinth by the confusion over the gift of tongues, that phenomenon by which people are able to speak ecstatic language. This is a phenomenon in Christendom which can cause considerable disunity. Paul's advice is most wholesome. He urged that people not covet that gift, but rather that they should earnestly strive to express themselves in love, even as our God spoke plainly to us of his love in Jesus Christ. There is no reason for us to live with any kind of communications gap among ourselves or be frustrated by the world's inability to carry on dialog. We are sent to speak reconciliation. We celebrate the miracle of God's love in Jesus Christ. By the power of the Spirit God enables us to speak and live by his love.

18

> The Lord created me at the beginning
>   of his work,
>   the first of his acts of old.
> Ages ago I was set up,
>   at the first, before the beginning
>   of the earth.
> When there were no depths I was
>   brought forth,
>   when there were no springs
>   abounding with water.
> Before the mountains had been
>   shaped,
>   before the hills, I was brought
>   forth;
> before he had made the earth
>   with its fields,
>   or the first of the dust of the
>   world.
> When he established the heavens,
>   I was there,
>   when he drew a circle on the
>   face of the deep,
> when he made firm the skies
>   above,
>   when he established the fountains
>   of the deep,
> when he assigned to the sea its
>   limit,
>   so that the waters might not
>   transgress his command,
> when he marked out the foundations
>   of the earth,
>   then I was beside him, like a
>   master workman;
> and I was daily his delight,
>   rejoicing before him always,
> rejoicing in his inhabited world
>   and delighting in the sons of
>   men.

Proverbs 8:22-31

Proverbs 8:22-31 *The Holy Trinity*

One in Three

Today we celebrate the Feast of the Holy Trinity. Much effort has gone into explaining the doctrine of the Holy Trinity, but most illustrations of the doctrine are flawed in one way or another. Quite often, too, the analogies that are used tend to make too little of the teaching. However we deal with this doctrine we must be careful not to explain away the mystery of God's great revelation of himself to us. Rather we confess the faith which is God's gift to us. We confess faith in the Triune God. We cannot explain the mystery of how God is three in one. We can confess the faith in the Holy Trinity, sing it, give witness to it as the manner in which we by faith experience God in God's relationship to us.

So central is the doctrine of the Holy Trinity that we confess it each Sunday, and it is the only doctrine which we commemorate with a special Sunday in the liturgical year. All other Sundays of the church year celebrate and recall events in the life of our Lord or in the life of God's people. We call ourselves Trinitarians, and we invoke the presence of the Holy Trinity each time we gather ourselves for worship or we make our own petitions in the privacy of our own devotions. On this day when we are mindful of how many people give testimony anew to the doctrine it is good for us to review the doctrine in our own hearts.

The Trinity of Time

The Lesson in Proverbs does not explicitly enunciate a doctrine of the Holy Trinity in the classical formula we use to confess it. Yet this passage in a rich and profound way helps us to recognize ways in which we experience God in other trinitarian manifestations. This portion of Proverbs is about Wisdom which the writer personifies as a partner of God in the creation of the universe. Wisdom is able to boast, "The Lord created me at the beginning of his work, the first of his acts of old."

Wisdom was "before the beginning" and recalls that Wisdom was extant before anything was created or called into existence. The past, Wisdom asserts, belongs to God. History is not simply happenstance, the way things fell into place by chance. God controlled the past, as God controls the present and will manage the future. All of this is dramatized for us in the life, death and resurrection of our Lord. All the events in the life of Jesus moved together to bring to a climax the act of reconciliation of the world in the cross of Christ. In the resurrection of Jesus God boldly demonstrated that the future belongs to God also. In God our lives are totally redeemed. The past and the present make us what we are; in the Risen Christ our future is secure. We do not live like some who deny history or like others who live as though there is no tomorrow.

The Trinity of Order

As the mysterious unity of the Trinity is evident in all of time we know that time is not wasted. All is redeemed. Christ can say, "I am the Alpha and Omega, the beginning and the end." (Revelations 21:6) Peter can write, "With the Lord one day is as a thousand years, and a thousand years as one day." (2 Peter 3:8) If God were not in control of the past, present and future, then history and time would be the victims of chance and of nature. As it is, however, the nature of the Trinity is equally manifest in the manner in which God has ordered things. Wisdom calls attention to the fact that God has given unity to the purpose, order, and course in the manner in which God does things. Wisdom uses words like "set up," "shaped," "established," "assigned," and "marked." All these words signal to us the manner in which God does things.

There is much we do not understand about the thoughts, ways and deeds of God. We are in no position to either analyze God or psychologize God. God gives us neither that right nor that kind of power. However, God does give us enough evidence, sufficient models, and ample experience to know that whatever God does works out for the welfare of those who love God, who are called according to God's purpose. (Romans 8:28) We know that best as we witness how God worked out divine purpose in the life of our Lord Jesus Christ. From that we know that the purpose, order and course of what God does is of God's good and gracious will. In Christ God has made known to us in all wisdom and insight the mystery of God's will. (Ephesians 1:9)

The Trinity of the Creation

The mystery of the unity of the Trinity is also manifest in the very creation itself. Wisdom confesses, "The Lord created me." God is the Creator. Wisdom observes how God created all the features of the universe. God shaped the mountains, brought forth the hills, laid on the fields, manufactured the dust from which it all came, established the heavens, drew a circle on the face of the deep, assigned the seas, gave orders to the waters, and marked out the foundation of the earth. Everything is a reflection of God. God's fingerprints are on everything, and everything exists only by God's fiat or permission.

The crowning glory of God's creative work was the people whom God fashioned out of love. Wisdom rejoices in the fact that she found particular delight in the sons and daughters who inhabit God's world. Thus the Creator, the creation, and the creatures within the creation are inseparable. We are dependent upon the Creator through the creation. The creation is dependent upon us to be its managers on behalf of the One who has created us. One does not have to be a pantheist to appreciate this unity. The pantheists equate God with the universe. In Christ we know better. Christ is the image of the invisible God. In Christ all things were created, and in Christ all things hold together. (Colossians 1:15-17) And we are one with Christ in faith.

The Unity of the Trinity

As we experience the trinitarian fashion in which God works in ordered manner in the creation and time, we are also conscious of the fact that we speak of God as a Trinity — Father, Son and Holy Spirit — one God, yet three distinct persons. There is no easy way in which we can explain the Trinity. People have used all manner of illustrations to describe the Holy Trinity, but usually they fall short of conveying the complexity of this phenomenon. Probably the best way for us to try and comprehend the unity of the Trinity is to examine our own personhood. We are also trinitarian. Back in the forties and fifties, because of the growing influence and importance of the behavioral sciences we made strong distinctions between physical, emotional and mental. Each of the professions worked together for the benefit of patients but were jealous of their individual areas and respectful of each other.

Today, however, we speak more and more of holistic health. We work harder at the business of dealing with the interrelations of the mind, spirit, and body. We are more conscious of the unity of the whole person and realize that we cannot deal with the individual without taking into account the trinitarian nature of the person. It were not as though each aspect of the person were a different manifestation of the whole person, but rather that the unity of the whole is made up of the three that are separate yet interdependent.

The Experience of the Trinity

As we can appreciate the complexity of our own trinitarian nature we can also get some insight into the nature of the Holy Trinity. If we hear people talking about the Trinity as though it sounds like there are three gods, then we know something is wrong. God is one. (Deuteronomy 6:4) Yet Jesus can say, "Believe me that I am in the Father and the Father in me." (John 13:11) He can also talk about whom the Father sends as proceeding from the Father as the Spirit of Truth to perform in the Spirit what Jesus had done in the flesh. (John 14 and 15)

In the same way Wisdom in the text before us speaks about this intimate relationship with the Creator. Wisdom identifies herself as a person. Theologians have termed this as a "hypostasis," which is to say that Wisdom is a reality as a person. Here Wisdom is not to be equated with ideas or thoughts that people normally talk about when they describe wisdom. Here Wisdom is a person of the Godhead who participates in the work of creation. We think of this Wisdom as the pre-existent Christ in the manner in which the Apostle Paul describes the cosmic Christ in the epistles to the Ephesians and the Colossians. In the same way the Hebrew Scriptures describe the presence of God over and over again as the presence of God's Spirit. The Hebrew Scriptures are as trinitarian as the Greek Scriptures. We cannot talk about God being present only as Father, or Son, or Spirit. God is one.

The Experience of Wisdom

For the writer of this portion of Proverbs the concept of Wisdom as a person of the Godhead has an important function in our lives. The Book of Proverbs has been a favorite of many because it appears to them to be a handy guide to living. It offers curious bits and pieces that one can reach for in many practical situations. Someone could use it as a farmer's almanac. Somebody else will use it for a marriage manual or guide to family living. However, this writer understands Wisdom in a much more profound way. Wisdom is not a collection of our best sayings or our best instructions for doing. Wisdom as a person is God's gift to us which becomes the basis for our ability to act in the freedom of his love and grace; it is also a gift to be pursued as we live and act under God's providence.

In this portion of Proverbs Wisdom discloses herself as the one who shared in the creative work of God which continues to this day among the inhabitants of the earth. It remains for us to live in the light of Wisdom's continuing caring role for us, that is, "delighting" in us. That is what the entire Book of Proverbs means to say to us. Rather than to think of the book as a series of laws and rubrics to be resorted to as the occasion demands, the Proverbs are intended to illustrate how those who love Wisdom, who trust God, would be able to react in the sight of the presence of Wisdom in their lives. This is to say that what we believe *about* God is not nearly so important as the fact that we believe *God*, that is, we can trust God to enable us to live and act in the divine assurance of love and grace.

Our Experience Today

We learn from Proverbs that to "know" God is to *trust* God — rather than to know *about* God. This is analogous to the manner in which we should understand our confessions or creeds. We are not to think of our creeds as laws or constitutions by which we abide in order to be accepted into the company of God. Rather, the creeds and confessions are the products of our faith. God creates the faith. The creeds are the responses, like doxologies, in which we affirm what God has done for us sinners in Christ Jesus.

The Apostles' Creed is a classic example of this expression of faith. The Creed makes no strained attempt to explain the nature of the Trinity, but rather confesses in faith and thanksgiving what God has done for us as Creator, Redeemer and Sanctifier. We assign to the Father the work of creation, to the Son, the work of redemption, and to the Holy Spirit the work of sanctification. Yet we know all are interdependent. We use the creeds and our confessions simply to accommodate our faith to the language that is available to us. What is important for us is that we rehearse the expression of this faith regularly. As the practitioner of any profession, art or sport knows, one must constantly fall back on the basics. So we of the faith fall back on the creeds to sustain us in crises, in daily life, and in relation to our neighbors. That is true wisdom.

Then Solomon stood before the altar of the Lord in the presence of all the assembly of Israel, and spread forth his hands toward heaven; and said, "O Lord, God of Israel, there is no God like thee, in heaven above or on earth beneath, keeping covenant and showing steadfast love to thy servants who walk before thee with all their heart.

"Likewise when a foreigner, who is not of thy people Israel, comes from a far country for thy name's sake (for they shall hear of thy great name, and thy mighty hand, and of thy outstretched arm), when he comes and prays toward this house, hear thou in heaven thy dwelling place, and do according to all for which the foreigner calls to thee; in order that all the peoples of the earth may know thy name and fear thee, as do thy people Israel, and that they may know that this house which I have built is called by thy name."

1 Kings 8:22-23, 41-43

1 Kings 8:22-23, 41-43 *Proper 4 (C)*
Pentecost 2 (L)
Corpus Christi (RC)

One in Prayer

Architecture in general reveals a great deal about what people have been thinking and doing. If we want to learn something about a given era or culture, we must study its architecture and arts. Probably the most dramatic revelation of the mood and accomplishment of a period is its architecture.

We think of how ancient Greek buildings demonstrate the reasoned approach of a philosophical people. Or we stand in awe of the medieval cathedrals that disclose the piety and heavenly aspirations of people who took seriously the thought of divine judgment. Some people believe that much of contemporary architecture betrays not only the high cost of building but also the sterility of contemporary thought.

Architecture and Worship

Every building committee has to wrestle with elemental questions of form and function. A congregational building committee has to do the same. How they answer those questions of form and function will depend upon whether they believe that the building should be designed to honor God, bring prestige to the congregation or simply give the congregation a meeting place. When one visits churches or looks at a book about church architecture one can understand how differently various building committees have understood their assignment.

Normally, when we walk into a church building we can tell if the architect was a worshiping Christian or not. Most often the clue is that one can detect whether the architect is used to seeing the worship in motion or not. If not, the chancel area when empty will look good on a multicolor postcard. If the architect is a worshiper, one will be able to see how the space is arranged to permit freedom of movement with the worship and to allow for color and pageantry. There are also other ways of understanding the function of church architecture. The Lesson for today helps us with that.

Solomon and Architecture

The Lesson is a portion of the lengthy prayer which King Solomon spoke as a royal priest at the dedication of the temple in Jerusalem. If you can recall, Solomon spent huge sums to bring the finest artisans and materials to build a shrine at Jerusalem. David, Solomon's father, had dreamed of erecting such a building to replace the tabernacle, the traveling tent edifice which the Children of Israel had used for many generations from the time of their wilderness wanderings. God, however, through the prophet Nathan, counseled David that he had used up so much of his energies in warring to extend the boundaries of the kingdom and to make it safe and inhabitable for Israel that he should not concern himself with building a temple. Rather David should concentrate on making peace and administering justice to get his realm in order.

Another generation could talk of building a temple, and David could be assured that God would bless this nation through David's descendants. Solomon picked up where David left off and generated great prosperity and prestige for Israel by building elaborate royal courts and this beautiful shrine in the capital city. Though it was not large, from all accounts it must have been startling in its beauty. Solomon employed some thirty thousand forced laborers to get the job done and completed the work after seven years. Solomon continued to build his royal complex in the precincts of the temple which then served also as a royal chapel in the capital city.

A Convenient Place

In the dedicatory prayer, however, Solomon recognizes an important fact. God does not need a building in which to be housed. No building, even as expensive, beautiful and stunning as the temple, can add anything to the prestige or glory of God. However, the temple could serve as a shrine, meeting place for God and people, to handle urgent and immediate concerns. The temple could serve as a convenient place for reconciliation between people. It could be a gathering place for the community to engage in an act of national repentance. The temple could be a place of refuge for the people to gather to offer prayers for relief from natural calamities of all sorts.

The people could also come to pray for relief from national disasters and international wars. Above all, the temple could be the place for the hearing of holy absolution, the reconciliation between God and man. All of these purposes for the existence of the building are cited in the longer version of the prayer which Solomon prayed on that solemn occasion. They were practical reasons. These are neither romantic nor pietistic notions about serving the glory of God by doing something for God, but they are the pragmatic and important matters in which the building dedicated to God is in reality placed in the service of people.

Built on a Solid Foundation

What was most important to the nature of the prayer that Solomon spoke was the basic assumption for his prayer. Solomon recognized and trusted the faithfulness of God. He rested his hope in the covenant that had been made with the Fathers, Abraham, Isaac, and Jacob. That covenant had been reaffirmed in the promises to David, Solomon's father. However, standing at the altar of this new edifice Solomon brought the Children of Israel into a new era. No longer were they a pilgrim people with whom God chose to dwell in a portable tent. Now God was willing to accommodate this people with the sign of God's presence, resident in a permanent place in the capital city. God had also indicated that the Davidic dynasty was to be the instrument by which God would rule over this people. The royal palace and the royal chapel were to be visible reminders of the faithfulness of God to the beloved, the chosen ones.

Whenever we read of the stories of the Hebrew people from the point of this dedication of temple forward, we have to be mindful of how deeply imbedded into the consciousness of this people is the sacramental character of the temple. All that had signaled the presence of God to them before this time — the tabernacle, the ark of the covenant, the pillar of cloud, the pillar of fire — were now incorporated into this building. There were no images in this building, no icons, no statues to represent God's presence. Only a veil, reminiscent of the veil that hid the shining countenance of Moses when he came down from Mount Sinai, hid from view of the people the actual Presence of the Holy One, Yahweh, in the holy of holies.

A Holy Presence

The importance of this presence of God at this site of the temple in Jerusalem was that it signaled the accessibility of God. God could be met. God could be reached by people who were in need of help and providence. More than that, this accessibility also guaranteed the grace of God. Solomon knew how lofty was the concept of God's Person. Yet he could pray, "Hearken thou to the supplication of thy people Israel, when they pray toward this place; yea, hear thou in heaven thy dwelling place; and when thou hearest, forgive." The God who promises to be present in this temple also fills the heavens with God's presence. But God is not a God afar off.

God is approachable, because God is the God of covenant and promise. God is willing to forgive. God provides a sacrificial system so that offerings are made for the sins of the people.

They do not have to offer their children or their virgins to placate this God. God has provided all the signs necessary to assure the people of grace. But God could be approached directly in prayer, because it was God's gracious nature to hear and to forgive. God in goodness would bend to the people to satisfy their needs and to grant them grace out of kindness.

A Place for All People

Not only does Solomon acknowledge this accessibility of a gracious God for the Hebrew people, but he indicates in his prayer that this accessibility is universal. He prays, "Likewise when a foreigner, who is not of thy people Israel, comes from a far country for thy name's sake . . . do according to all for which the foreigner calls to thee; in order that all the people of the earth may know thy name and fear thee." Here is one more sign of how the universality of God's grace is so strongly imprinted in the Hebrew Scriptures. The temple included the court of the Gentiles so that the stranger in the gate might make his way to Yahweh. There were a multitude of other customs, signs, and trials that should make that clear for the people. Yet we know how elitist and exclusive the people were to come at different times.

We are no different. We like to think that the New Testament writings introduced the universality of the Gospel of our Lord Jesus Christ. As surely as Solomon prayed that the temple was built as a house of prayer for all people, we preach that our Lord Jesus Christ died for all people. Yet we think with shame on the manner in which the Christian church's history is blemished with the record of segregation and exclusivity from the beginning. Now, in this day of civil rights, we are embarrassed again when Christian institutions defy even the law of the land with the claim that they are upholding a scriptural position when they defend their rights to segregate. Their attitude also defies the spirit of this great dedicatory prayer of Solomon.

A Good Example

The Holy Gospel for today is a perfect illustration of what Solomon prays in his prayer. The centurion whose servant was ill apparently was one of those strangers who had come to the temple as a proselyte. He befriended the Jews when he built a synagogue for them. Now he makes his prayer to our Lord Jesus through intermediaries. For us the inference is clear. Jesus is the one who has come to replace the temple as the sign of God's mercy and grace for us. The Lord Jesus by his suffering, death, resurrection and ascension is for us the one who fills heaven and earth with his presence and makes God accessible for us.

The centurion had only the messianic presence of Jesus to go by. But our Lord did not disappoint him. He healed the servant and then paid this tribute of enormous respect to the faith of one who did not come out of Israel. That is comfort for us. If we are embarrassed for our own bigotry or the prejudice of the church at times, we know God forgives that, too. But more than that God is also actively hearing the prayers of people who test grace with their prayers, no matter who, where, or what they may be. What is so good about that is that we know God will always hear our prayers. God will hear us even when we feel like we are strangers to God.

After this the son of the woman, the mistress of the house, became ill; and his illness was so severe that there was no breath left in him. And she said to Elijah, "What have you against me, O man of God? You have come to me to bring my sin to remembrance, and to cause the death of my son!" And he said to her, "Give me your son." And he took him from her bosom, and carried him up into the upper chamber, where he lodged, and laid him upon his own bed. And he cried to the Lord, "O Lord my God, hast thou brought calamity even upon the widow with whom I sojourn, by slaying her son?" Then he stretched himself upon the child three times, and cried to the Lord, "O Lord my God, let this child's soul come into him again." And the Lord hearkened to the voice of Elijah; and the soul of the child came into him again, and he revived. And Elijah took the child, and brought him down from the upper chamber into the house and delivered him to his mother; and Elijah said, "See, your son lives." And the woman said to Elijah, "Now I know that you are a man of God, and that the word of the Lord in your mouth is truth."

1 Kings 17:17-24

1 Kings 17:17-24

Proper 5 (C)
Pentecost 3 (L)
Ordinary Time 10 (RC)

One Word of Truth

There is a poignant story that has a great deal to say about the Lesson appointed for this day. The story is about the fellow who was caught in the deep waters of torrential rains. The man was standing in water to his knees when folks came by in a boat and asked him to jump in. He said, "No, I'll wait. The Lord will provide." A while later he was standing in water up to his chest, and rescuers came by in a speed boat and urged him to jump in. He said, "No. The Lord will provide." When he was standing in water up to his neck people flew over him in a helicopter. They threw a line down to him and told him to grab on. He said, "No. The Lord will provide." Of course, you know what happened. The waters rose, inundated the man, and he drowned.

The man died and went to heaven. When he got there he immediately registered a complaint. He explained how firmly he had believed, only to be disappointed. He was ushered to the throne of the Almighty where he reiterated his complaint, "How could you let me down, when I kept believing that you would provide?" The Almighty answered, "Dummy, who do you think sent the two boats and the helicopter?" That story has a profound meaning. Do we not all fail to see how the Lord is operative daily in our lives working through the means that are everywhere about us? It is by faith that we discern that God is working to provide for us and to protect us.

No Fairy Tales

It is remarkable that our children are able to make such discernments. Our children come to Sunday church school and church classes to learn stories from the Scriptures that are lessons about what God had done for his people in ancient Israel. They also learn the stories about what our Lord Jesus accomplished in his ministry. At home they learn nursery rhymes and fairy tales on the laps of their fathers and their mothers. In school they read fables and heroic tales. Yet they are able to distinguish between the real and the fanciful. Children can tell the difference between fairy tales and the miracle stories of the Scriptures.

The early church had to make those kinds of distinctions also. Many stories circulated in the early church about the early life of Jesus that were fanciful tales to enhance the character of Jesus as the all powerful Son of God. Such stories were also fabricated about the powers of the disciples after our Lord Jesus had ascended on high. The church in time rejected those stories which had the fairy tale quality to them and those stories became known as the apocrypha of the New Testament and were never accepted into the canon of the Scriptures. Today we have a good opportunity to examine the manner in which we ourselves can test the validity of a miracle story with the Lesson before us.

Elijah, an Unpopular Hero

The story is about one of the most famous heroes in the Scripture. Elijah is the prophet who stands tall in the lineup of the prophets. Elijah worked the Northern Kingdom, Israel, in the eighth century before Christ. He worked that area at a time when the apostasy of the northern kingdom was rampant, and the worship of Baal had become almost a national religion under the rule of King Ahab and Jezebel. Because Elijah had successfully challenged the priests of Baal to a contest and won, he had to flee for his life. You recall what the contest had been. The priests of Baal were not able successfully to invoke their god to consume their sacrifice. Elijah, however, was confident that God would ignite the sacrifice that he had soaked in water. And God did. Because the people still refused to repent, God sent a famine upon the land, and Ahab and Jezebel put a bounty on the head of Elijah.

Elijah fled to an alien town, Zarephath, where he found refuge in the home of a widow. There God provided for the widow, her son, and Elijah with resources that did not fail. This was a difficult time for Elijah. He was holed up in this place. If he had achieved any victory over the prophets of Baal, it appeared to be a hollow victory. What good did that serve now? Ahab and Jezebel appeared to be hardened in their disbelief and refused to yield to the message of the prophet. If there was any comfort for Elijah at this time, it was that God was content to sustain the prophet on the meager provisions of the widow. That was small comfort, indeed, in the face of the enormous unsolved problems that plagued the land.

Trouble for the Prophet

On top of that, the widow's son takes ill, "and his illness was so severe that there was no breath left in him." That certainly does not help matters. This widow is no Hebrew. Elijah is in strange territory. The woman was now terrified by his presence. She may have thrilled to the manner in which this household has been sustained in the famine. However all during that time she may also have had to wonder why this was happening to her. Is this some kind of witchcraft or magic? Now when her son becomes so violently ill, she reasons that it is because this man of God is there to expose her sin and bring judgment upon her life and her home.

The widow reasons that the cause for her son's death is her sin. The occasion for his illness was the judgment that the prophet had brought to her door. Even Elijah feels that burden along with her. He complains to God. "O Lord my God, hast thou brought calamity even upon the widow with whom I sojourn, by slaying her son?" Elijah is perplexed. What kind of a development was this? He wondered, too, about the causal relationship between his presence and the death of this son. God had to be responsible. What an anxious moment this was for the widow and for Elijah! We all know that kind of time. When something goes wrong, we wonder what we have done wrong to deserve the judgment and wrath of God. We cringe when we think of how God could punish us, so what goes wrong must be a sign of God's displeasure with us.

A Miracle of Life

Having expressed his chagrin at the situation, Elijah also prayed over the child as he stretched himself over the child three times and cried to the Lord, "O Lord my God, let this child's soul come into him again." And the prayer was heard. The child was revived. Every one of us can say that Elijah employed good technique here. He followed routine for code blue. Obviously he was pushing upon the child's chest and practiced mouth to mouth resuscitation. He supplied wind for the child's lungs and forced the air to resume natural breathing. Elijah was able to bring the child down from the upper chamber and hand him over to his mother and say, "See, your son lives." That is the simple explanation of how a quick-thinking person was able to rescue a life with emergency treatment. However, that is not how the widow interpreted it. She said, "Now I know that you are a man of God, and that the word of the Lord in your mouth is truth."

The widow perceived that more had happened than that Elijah was some kind of paramedic. She believed that he was a man of God who had life-giving power. He was filled with the breath of life. He had the power of God to give life as God himself gave life to the first creatures when he breathed into them the breath of life and they became living beings.

Elijah had given the breath of life from his own being, therefore the words which came from him must also be life-giving. The word of the prophet must be the truth of God. Elijah had done the natural thing, but for him the natural thing was also the means by which God works. The woman was the beneficiary of this natural action, but she also discerned that the hand of God was in this matter. God worked through the natural means to accomplish his purpose.

God Still Gives Life

That we ought to be able to see. And the man standing in the water should have known that God was supplying the rescue missions. But how do we explain the times, the many times, when life is not saved or restored? We have all read of cults of people who await the resurrection of the dead. There are many people who insist that the surest sign of God's outpouring of his Spirit in the world today in a Pentecostal revival is the resurrection of the dead. The way to give certainty to the Word today is resurrection of the dead by prayer. You have heard of such bizarre stories of people failing to bury their dear ones, because they are sure that they will rise by a certain date through the power of prayer.

At the same time we hear of the many successful stories of open heart surgery as well as transplants and other exotic and sophisticated surgery that have lengthened the lives of people, literally brought people back from death or through the valley of death. Then we also think of the heartache that has come to many, many devout Christian people who have lost dear ones and their beloved in spite of their faithful and fervent prayers. What shall we say to them when the breath of life is not restored? Could it be that faith is in vain or that the Word is not truth for them, or that no person of God is present in their lives?

The Importance of the Resurrection

Certainly the answer to those questions should be easy. *We* know that we have a gracious and loving God who is present with us at all times. We do not have the answers as to why some are healed and others not. On any given Sunday as a congregation we could be praying in thanksgiving for someone who has been healed and in the next petition we could be praying for the comfort of a family who has lost a dear one after a long hard struggle in prayer and hope. How we deal with the situation when death does come is illustrated for us in the Holy Gospel for today. Jesus demonstrates his sympathy for the widow at Nain who has just lost her son. He tells her not to weep. He stops the funeral procession, and touches the bier, an act forbidden by law because death was considered unclean. He addresses the young man. "Young man, I say to you arise." The young man did, and Jesus gave him to his mother. The people, filled with fear, confess that a prophet had risen among them. Just as the woman at Zarephath recognized Elijah as the Spirit filled the prophet whose words gave life, the people so recognize Jesus.

However, it was precisely because the people thought that Jesus might be Elijah returned to the earth, because they thought of him popularly as a prophet, that he himself was put to death. Jesus resuscitated the young man at Nain. He did not employ Elijah's technique, only the power of his words. Yet Jesus had power over death. That was what he wanted to demonstrate while he was yet among the people as a prophet. However, when his life was taken from him, when undeserved death came to him he relied upon his faith in the Heavenly Father to be the means by which he would be raised from the dead. And God so raised him from the dead. God raised him as God also promises to raise us from the dead.

The Ultimate of Life

Therein lies the answer as to how we must handle the matter when death comes. If God chooses to lengthen our days, because God spares us in an emergency by resuscitation by some paramedic, or if God chooses to snatch us from the door of death by some exotic surgery, or if God cheats death for us by the introduction of some newly developed internal medicine, good. The honor is God's. Then God has been among us and God has used the means of medicine as the lifeboats to rescue us from death. If, however, we die, God has been present to satisfy that problem too.

Once more God did so through the very natural means of death. God saved us from death by dying. We could not ask more. That is the most radical kind of surgery God could perform. By the death on the *cross* God cut out the cancers of sin, God removed the threat of eternal judgment and gave back to us the breath of life. That is the ultimate for us. Because we know and believe that to be true because of what God has done in our Lord Jesus Christ, we can trust God to work in our lives under the worst possible circumstances, and we are confident that nothing can separate us from God's love and the life that God gives us. When death comes God has prepared us well. We can deal with it on any terms, because we already have conquered it by faith and life is ours.

Ahab told Jezebel all that Elijah had done, and how he had slain all the prophets with the sword. Then Jezebel sent a messenger to Elijah, saying, "So may the gods do to me, and more also, if I do not make your life as the life of one of them by this time tomorrow." Then he was afraid, and he arose and went for his life, and came to Beer-sheba, which belongs to Judah, and left his servant there.

But he himself went a day's journey into the wilderness, and came and sat down under a broom tree; and he asked that he might die, saying, "It is enough; now, O Lord, take away my life; for I am no better than my fathers." And he lay down and slept under a broom tree; and behold, an angel touched him, and said to him, "Arise and eat." And he looked, and behold, there was at his head a cake baked on hot stones and a jar of water. And he ate and drank, and lay down again. And the angel of the Lord came again a second time, and touched him, and said, "Arise and eat, else the journey will be too great for you." And he arose, and ate and drank, and went in the stength of that food forty days and forty nights to Horeb the mount of God.

1 Kings 19:1-8

1 Kings 19:1-8

Proper 6 (C)
Pentecost 4 (L)
Ordinary Time 11 (RC)

One Lonely Prophet

Who of us has not come to that moment when one feels like throwing in the towel? There are times when we feel so emotionally exhausted that we cannot go on. Or we may feel so frustrated that we may come to the conclusion that there is no use for going on. Some of us are more easily depressed than others. However, none of us can escape those feelings of depression that set in when we have no sense of accomplishment. Luther suffered from severe and chronic depression. One would think that the liberation that Luther experienced in the Gospel would have completely freed him from the misery of the headaches, the ringing in the ears, and the attacks of despair that came upon him.

However, as the amount of the work increased for Luther, so also did he become more deeply aware of how great a battle he was fighting. At night a cloud of terrible sadness often enveloped him as he contemplated the enemies that surrounded him. The burden of the reformation work increased the personal burdens and pain he had to bear. The most difficult feature of the pain that he had to endure was the loneliness Luther sensed as he had to make grave decisions that made him feel that he was going against the church and the world. He was not the first to feel this way. That was the occupational hazard of being prophetic. Elijah was an outstanding example of the lonely prophet.

The Victim of Retaliation

What created a desperate situation for Elijah was the fact that he had earned the indignation of Jezebel, the Queen of Israel. That beautiful and brilliant woman had imported the system of Baal worship with an entire complement of priests from her homeland of Phoenicia. Elijah had won his famous contest with the priests of Baal, had slain them and had proclaimed victory for Yahweh. One would have thought that the entire nation would have been brought to its knees along with King Ahab and Queen Jezebel. However, that is not always how it works.

The freedom of the Gospel also produces reactions that are negative and sometimes openly hostile. In this case, Jezebel was bent on retaliation. She was convinced that Elijah had to go. She sent a message to Elijah vowing, "So may the gods do to me, and more also, if I do not make your life as the life of one of them (the slain prophets of Baal) by this time tomorrow." Jezebel did not believe the word of the prophet and was not going to worship Yahweh, who had given evidence of the superiority of Yahweh over Baal. She was determined to do away with this prophet who preached so easily and confidently about Yahweh. Yahweh had brought out the worst in her. What should have evoked faith from her aroused only anger, hatred, and evil.

The Prophet is Despondent

The prophet did not take the threat of Jezebel lightly. He ran for his life. He did not stop until he reached the southern border of Israel. At Beer-Sheba, which belonged to Judah, he ditched his servant, so that he could travel on without being concerned for the safety of the additional person. He did not waste much time and moved on another whole day's journey in the wilderness. Finally in sheer exhaustion Elijah came to rest in the shade of a broom tree. A broom tree is so named because it does not offer much more shade than a broom, getting to be about ten feet tall and being rather skimpy with its foliage. However, it was the best resting place Elijah could find under the circumstances, and nothing was going to offer him much comfort for the way in which he felt. Frustrated, hurt, frightened, and emotionally drained, Elijah is at the end of his tether.

Elijah feels that there is absolutely no use for going on. He complains to God that he has had it. After all, how much can a person take, and how much should one be expected to take? Things are so bad that Elijah wants to die. He pleads with God, "It is enough; now, O Lord, take away my life; for I am no better than my fathers." In spite of his heroic efforts at Carmel, Elijah had gained nothing. Elijah certainly had to be disgusted with the people who failed to rally to his cause. He might have expected the reactions of Ahab and Jezebel, but then he probably also had hoped that they would have a change of heart. And what about God's reaction. Where was God in all this? If God could do no better for him, what was the use? He might just as well lie down and die.

A Sacramental Meal

Well, Elijah had a good snooze anyway. The sleep was refreshment for him and allowed his emotions to subside. He was awakened by an angel. We do not know in what kind of form or appearance the angel came. Was it simply a friendly stranger who took pity on the obviously distraught pilgrim? Was it a local native who kept an eye out for people who would run the danger of being scorched by the sun in the wilderness? At any rate, the kindly angelic figure had provided a cake "baked on hot stones and a jar of water."

The good sleep and the sight of food and drink helped Elijah to forget about his death wishes, and the will to live returned. He ate and drank and returned to his place of slumber to get some more rest. He did not suffer from anorexia.

Nor was he belligerent at this point. He did not become hysterical, but he appeared to be one whose nervous exhaustion had drained him of all energy. The meal had sacramental quality to it. Elijah had prayed to die, and the meal offered him life. Elijah had assumed that his whole life had been of no value, and the meal was offered as an assurance that God loved him and would provide for him. Elijah had thought it was all over, and the meal suggested a new beginning. Elijah's desperation led him to believe that he was all alone. The meal assured him that God was with him.

A Second Meal

At this point the prophet had become docile. Most of us have seen this happen to people who have been emotionally drained. After a deep depression or seizure of hysteria they may respond in a quiet and meek manner to whatever ministrations are given them. They are by no means over their deep sense of desperation or frustration. However, they are completely devoid of the strength to cope on their own. They need care and attention. At this point Elijah is such a patient. He is a shell of his former self. This is not the prophet who singlehandedly had been willing to take on the royal court as well as the whole state establishment of baal worship. Right now the prophet needed someone to furnish the old spark, to give something back to him that would relight the flame of passion he once had for the causes of Yahweh.

God did not disappoint Elijah. "The angel of the Lord came again a second time, and touched him, and said, 'Arise and eat, else the journey will be too great for you.' " God ministers to the prophet with tender loving care. Elijah was not ready to go on another journey without the proper nourishment. The second meal once again is sacramental in character. God gives of love, providence and grace as the prophet is nourished through bread and drink. This time the sustenance of the meal renews the prophet so that he was able to go "in the strength of that food forty days and forty nights to Horeb the mount of God." Horeb was Mount Sinai. God was preparing Elijah for a great religious confrontation and experience such as Moses had known on the very same turf where Moses had been.

The Long Ordeal

Probably most of us have wondered what people like Moses and Elijah did for forty days in the mountain. For us activists that seems to be an inordinate amount of time to be locked into a retreat. Yet when we look at these larger-than-life heroic figures we realize how much time God had to consume in preparing them for what God wanted them to be. These people were not only brilliant but their emotions matched their brains. They felt deeply. They identified with the foibles and weaknesses of their people as well as with mercies and goodness of God. Their minds and hearts were the arenas in which the sympathies they felt for both God and people met.

God had to take time with these people who were as delicate as they were strong, who had doubts as well as enormous faith. God had to take the same kind of time with Jesus, God's Son, who spent forty days and nights in the wilderness. God had to take time with Luther at Coburg Hall while the Reformer waited out the results of the Diet of Augsburg. God took time to prepare Abraham Lincoln so that he could bear the burdens of this nation in one of its most critical hours. God not only calls the prophets, but God makes the prophets. God takes time in shaping and making them to fit the work that God calls them to do.

How God Deals with Us

However, we should not think that God is attentive only to heroic figures or that God spends that kind of time only with the people who amount to a great deal. God does the same for us. God knows that the little people have their doubts, too. God knows we have frustrations. God knows we suffer from depressions. God knows we have death wishes, that we would just as soon give everything up at times. That is why God chose to send Jesus as the greatest of all prophets to bear all of those burdens we endure. Jesus suffered the same hardships and disappointments that came to Elijah and all the other prophets like him. However, our Lord also suffered death at the hands of the enemy. Jesus' death wish was most appropriate. He was willing to die that he might overcome the enemy. By his resurrection from the dead the Lord Jesus made it possible that we do not have to be despondent in the face of death itself.

Yet God knew we would still have our bad days and our ugly moments. For that our Lord gave us the sacramental meal of his body and blood under the forms of bread and wine so that we might be refreshed and "go in strength." God has also given us our mount of refuge, our Mount Horeb, in the Word. We can have our rendezvous with God in the Word which is the source of our worship, our devotion, our study, and our prayers. God is willing to attend to our needs, nurse our emotional hurts, wait us out and prepare us to be the witnesses to the love of our Lord Jesus Christ. God makes us Christians. God fashions us as the children of the Kingdom. God can even make us prophetic.

A Legend on How God Does It

There is a Hasidic legend that makes the point. Once upon a time three Hasidim made a pilgrimage to spend high holy days with the rabbi of Lublin, Poland. They went without food or money. Soon they became weak. They decided that if one of them would pose as a rabbi they would be treated well in the villages. Sure enough, when they came to a little village, the innkeeper took care of them but also told them of his small son who was dying. What else could the pretender do but go with him to see the son. The next morning they went on in a carriage furnished by the grateful father. They were thrilled to hear the great rabbi in Lublin and returned in ecstasy after the holy days passed.

However, the three were fearful as they had to approach the innkeeper. Much to their surprise he greeted them with thanksgiving and reported that the son had been made well. When they were alone, the pretender revealed to his colleagues that when he had seen the son he prayed to God in confession that he was a pretender. But he also argued with God that if the child died the father would probably think that the rabbis can do nothing. So he prayed that God heal the son not for the sake of the pretender, but for the faith of the father. So it is that God works. God works in spite of us, in spite of the doubts of an Elijah, a Moses or a Luther, or even our doubts. Yet God cares for us and uses us to accomplish the divine will in the world.

And there he came to a cave, and lodged there; and behold, the word of the Lord came to him, and he said to him, "What are you doing here, Elijah?" He said, "I have been very jealous for the Lord, the God of hosts; for the people of Israel have forsaken thy covenant, thrown down thy altars, and slain thy prophets with the sword; and I, even I only, am left; and they seek my life, to take it away." And he said, "Go forth, and stand upon the mount before the Lord." And behold, the Lord passed by, and a great and strong wind rent the mountains, and broke in pieces the rocks before the Lord, but the Lord was not in the wind; and after the wind an earthquake; but the Lord was not in the earthquake; and after the earthquake a fire, but the Lord was not in the fire; and after the fire a still small voice. And when Elijah heard it, he wrapped his face in his mantle and went out and stood at the entrance of the cave. And behold, there came a voice to him, and said, "What are you doing here, Elijah?" He said, "I have been very jealous for the Lord, the God of hosts; for the people of Israel have forsaken thy covenant, thrown down thy altars, and slain thy prophets with the sword; and I, even I only, am left; and they seek my life, to take it away."

1 Kings 19:9-14

1 Kings 19:9-14 *Proper 7 (C)*
Pentecost 5 (L)
Ordinary Time 12 (RC)

One Still Small Voice

Poll after poll is conducted to explore attitudes of people toward American institutions. The polls are consistent in revealing that the average American has lost confidence in those American institutions which were once cherished bulwarks of our way of life. The current disillusionment with our institutions can be traced back to the fifties, "the golden age of the organization." Then we placed more confidence in institutions and organizations than we should have. In the sixties our institutions were all but dismantled, because all kinds of people reminded us that the institutions had failed them, abused them, or neglected them.

Today people have remained skeptical of the institutions. They have preferred to find their own solutions to their problems. They continue to challenge the authority of institutions and to preserve the right to do for themselves as they will. Given the temper of our times we can well appreciate the story of the prophet Elijah, who felt much the same way about institutions. His negative feelings about church and state in his day will give us an insight into our attitudes today. However, what will be even more helpful for us is to see how God reacted to the expressions of the prophet.

Elijah is Depressed

One can readily understand Elijah's distress and depression. Working in the Northern Kingdom, Elijah had confronted and rebuked King Ahab and Queen Jezebel at every turn they took in the road from leading the people away from the covenant and promises of God. Ahab had been an ambitious king of considerable talent. He had built the power and wealth of Israel into an enviable position. He had built alliances, one of them through marriage to the Phoenician princess Jezebel, a woman generously endowed with beauty and brains.

Jezebel came to Israel to fascinate and trouble the people with her flair for the dramatic and her practice of Phoenician culture and religion. She imported priests of Baal and almost succeeded in making Baal worship the state religion. It was this effort that Elijah had successfully challenged. If Jezebel had a flair for the dramatic, so did Elijah. In his well-known contest with the priests of Baal, Elijah won hands down as his sacrifice was consumed by fire from heaven. Elijah then ordered the prophets of Baal killed. Ahab was impressed, but not Jezebel. She vowed to destroy Elijah and began the manhunt for him. Elijah was frightened and ran for cover. In the dark shelter of a cave he was confronted by God.

Elijah's Gripe

The word which comes to Elijah is a question. What is he doing hiding in a cave? What is the bold prophet afraid of now? How is it that the one who had faced up to the power of the throne now cowers at the word from the queen? Elijah is ready with an answer. "I have been very jealous for the Lord, the God of hosts; for the people of Israel have forsaken thy covenant, thrown down thy altars, and slain thy prophets with the sword; and I, even I only, am left; and they seek my life to take it away." The answer sounds like a legitimate gripe. Where is God's justice in this situation? Elijah had been faithful to God in every way. But to what good? A ruthless government had put him to flight, and the people whom he had tried to save from meaningless idolatry were steeped in their sin.

Persecution had won out, and Elijah felt himself to be the singular voice left against all this unfaithfulness of his people and his state. That is a common complaint today. God-fearing people see that most everything seems to be out of control. Evil appears to have the upper hand. Righteousness does not win out. Bad people not only seem to have all the fun, but they also have all the power. God's people seemingly shrink in numbers, influence, and authority to the point where a God-fearing man has every right to believe that he is left all alone in the world as the last child of God left on the planet. We all know the feeling. The same thoughts come to us all in one way or another.

God's Surprise

The answer comes in a strange way to Elijah. The prophet is prompted to go out to Mount Horeb, which is Sinai, where God has revealed himself to Moses. There he senses the presence of God, but not in the manner he would have expected. A shattering wind passes by him destroying rocks, but God is not in the wind. Then comes an earthquake in which God is not present. Then comes a fire, but God is not in the fire. Then comes the still small voice, and he recognizes the presence of God. All of this was God's way of revealing to Elijah that he does not always come in a mighty show of power as we expect. Rather God comes in hidden ways.

God's presence is not shown in brilliant displays of might in history. Nor is the effect of the still small voice to mean that God is without power. However, the wind, the earthquake, and the fire are God's. Elijah is to know that God comes as a friend and that God is active in our lives in unexpected ways. Luther liked to talk of the masks of God. By that Luther meant to say that God comes behind a mask. These masks are the commonplace of life rather than the spectacular. To be sure, God can vent wrath upon the world, and does. But to God's children, God comes as a friend. Furthermore, God comes to us in a voice, in a word of revelation to make clear to us God's intention and plan for us. For Elijah the still small voice was the voice of God's love.

The Voice for Us

The still small voice ought to be meaningful for us also. All of us know how to engage in spiritual pouting. We make out excuses for hiding from the world or the obligations that the Word lays upon us. We can curl up in our smug self-satisfaction and convince ourselves that we are the only faithful left in the world. We wonder why it is that God does not exhibit dissatisfaction with the world. If we had our way God would shatter the unfaithful, swallow them up in hell, or consume them with hell fires. We hear the complaint with great regularity, "Where have all the hellfire preachers gone?" "Why don't the preachers preach the Law any more?" "We sure don't have thunder in the sermons any more." That kind of criticism, however, normally is based on the same kind of assumption Elijah made. Such criticism stems from a notion that we can afford to have God vent spleen on the world and we alone would be left to withstand it.

The still small voice comes, however, to remind us that our chief sin is our unwillingness to trust God. Elijah was depressed, was hiding, and failed in his courage because he did not at that moment believe that God was in charge of a messed up world that permitted evil to have its day. Elijah could get his courage back, but not when he would see what God would do to Elijah's enemies. His courage would return when he had confidence and could trust God. Elijah's courage failed not because there was not enough law around. Elijah was weak because he was counting on his own resources as a child of God and that was not enough. Clearly his own moxie failed him. He needed the still small voice.

The Voice Returns

The still small voice comes to Elijah and asks him a second time what he is doing. Once again he repeats the essence of his disappointment, disillusionment, and despair. God does not concede the rationale behind Elijah's complaint. God does not engage in a great deal of dialogue or nondirective counseling to handle the situation. God does not give in to the complaints of the faithful prophet. No matter how reasonable the complaint seemed to Elijah it had no basis before God. Elijah was viewing his situation in the light of how the world measures success.

When we have so little reason to keep faith with the institutions of church and state because of the failures we see, God does not want us to lose faith in the Word. We are readily discouraged when we uncover corruption in government, when there is scandal in law enforcement agencies, and when government appears to ignore the ethical and all good sense of morality. At such a time we need to remember that our God is still in charge. God rules with either Democrats or Republicans in power. (Some of us have a hard time believing that!) He rules in the world when tensions build in the Mideast, just as they did in the day of Elijah. God rules in the world with detente and without it.

We Have our Orders

God came to Elijah to remind Elijah that the game was not over. God comes to us in the same way. We are to go on. We are to choose and work with the best people we are able to find. We are to work and sweat for making the world the best possible place that we can. In all of that God rules. God presses upon the world for us to put forth our best effort, and at the same time, God desires that people look up for help, guidance and strength. Elijah was prevented from playing God by the still small voice. Instead, he was being invited by God to trust God's ultimate rule. We can say the same for the church. The church may appear to be of no consequence in the world, yet it is there hidden in the world. The church may not appear to make large ripples upon the sea of history, but in the end it alone survives the ravages of time.

We can understand this still small voice best when we see how effectively our God worked for us in the life and ministry of our Lord Jesus Christ. Silently God stole into the world in the person of the Child of Bethlehem. Quietly Jesus worked among people and preached the revolutionary Gospel which finally brought Jesus to the cross. Yet by the death and the resurrection of this Son, God worked out salvation of humankind. All happened so quietly no one could believe what God was doing. God worked in such a homely fashion in the life of this Son that they could not believe this was God's way of reclaiming the human race.

God not only identified with our humanity, but God also suffered what all humanity has to suffer all the way to death. When God raised Jesus from the dead God proved the still small voice could be trusted. We can trust that God's way of working things out in the world in spite of us and for us is absolutely trustworthy. We shall find that the resource for ministry in God's service always derives only from the still small voice of God's gracious Gospel. Encouraged by God's grace, we are free to work with confidence. The point is that we are to look to God for the still small voice for help and strength.

And the Lord said to him, "Go, return on your way to the wilderness of Damascus; and when you arrive, you shall anoint Hazael to be king over Syria; and Jehu the son of Nimshi you shall anoint to be king over Israel; and Elisha the son of Shaphat of Abelmeholah you shall anoint to be prophet in your place. And him who escapes from the sword of Hazael shall Jehu slay; and him who escapes from the sword of Jehu shall Elisha slay. Yet I will leave seven thousand in Israel, all the knees that have not bowed to Baal, and every mouth that has not kissed him."

So he departed from there, and found Elisha the son of Shaphat, who was plowing, with twelve yoke of oxen before him, and he was with the twelfth. Elijah passed by him and cast his mantle upon him. And he left the oxen, and ran after Elijah, and said, "Let me kiss my father and my mother, and then I will follow you." And he said to him, "Go back again; for what have I done to you?" And he returned from following him, and took the yoke of oxen, and slew them, and boiled their flesh with the yokes of the oxen, and gave it to the people, and they ate. Then he arose and went after Elijah, and ministered to him.

1 Kings 19:15-21

1 Kings 19:15-21

Proper 8 (C)
Pentecost 6 (L)
Ordinary Time 13 (RC)

One Call to Follow

Most of us grown folk can remember the importance of finding mother home when we came in from school. We may recall the dreadfully lonely feeling of coming in when Mother was gone to the store or was absent for any other reason. That same kind of feeling can come over us yet when we are alone for some reason. There are worse kinds of loneliness. There is the terror one feels when one has done something wrong and has to worry about facing the music. That is a lonely feeling we do not enjoy, but at the same time we may feel better off being alone rather than having to make the big confrontation. An even lonelier feeling comes when something dreadful has happened to us, and there is no one to help. At such a time we may be frantic in the hope that someone will come to help.

The loneliest feeling of all is the feeling of being left out. Somehow as little people we could sense that all the other experiences of loneliness may have been by accident. However, when we are left out, that is by design. Some people have passed us over or passed us by deliberately. We can hope that the other forms of loneliness can be remedied by someone coming home or coming to the rescue. But to be left out means that some people did not care in the first place, that we have been rejected, and the chances are that nobody will care. That is the kind of loneliness that Elijah experienced, but it was even intensified, because he believed that God had deserted him.

The Prophet

It is not difficult to understand why Elijah would feel deserted. From all appearances he was deserted. Elijah had singlehandedly taken on both the religious and the government establishments. A few weeks ago we met him in the home of the widow at Zarephath. He had taken refuge there, because he needed to hide out from King Ahab and Queen Jezebel who had put a bounty upon Elijah's head. We realize how desperate Elijah had felt at that time because he had been exiled from his people and from his home. Elijah was in hiding because he had delivered to Ahab the word from the Lord that the famine in the land would come as a punishment for their idolatry of Baal.

After Elijah raised the son of the widow at Zarephath he came out of hiding to confront Ahab. On the way to Ahab he met Obadiah who had been keeping some of the faithful in hiding also. But only Elijah has the courage to face Ahab, who dubs Elijah "the troubler of Israel." It was then that Elijah challenged the prophets of Baal to that great contest to see whose God would help them. Elijah had to flee once more. In loneliness he complained to God, in loneliness he flees to the desert, in loneliness God provides for him at the Brook Kerioth. In loneliness he retreats to a cave, where we meet him again.

Alone and Depressed

In that kind of loneliness one can appreciate Elijah's disappointment and depression. He complains to God, "I have been very jealous for the Lord, the God of hosts; for the people of Israel have forsaken thy covenant, thrown down thy altars and slain thy prophets with the sword; and I even I only, am left; and they seek my life to take it away." That is a legitimate complaint. In reality Elijah was asking the Lord, what was the good of it all? Where is the payoff for being faithful and risking your life for the sake of what you believe God wants you to do and what you believe is the truth? Elijah in effect was saying that he had done his part for God. His being very jealous for God meant that he had acted on behalf of God in the way in which the prophets normally said God had acted on behalf of Israel. The Hebrew word that is translated "jealous" here primarily means the color that is produced in the face as a result of violent emotion. It suggests becoming "red with dye." That emotion is the same as when a husband becomes jealous for his wife, or a wife for her husband, because they are zealous for them.

Elijah had behaved as a lover. He had acted as the representative of God's love for Israel. He had expressed the faithfulness of God over and over again through the interpretation of the covenant between God and Israel. But God's people had broken the relationship. They had found other lovers in the idols and prophets of Baal. Now Elijah felt that he was the only one left. Elijah was left holding the bag. He had been faithful in every way, but no good had come of it. What was the use? Elijah's reward was that the people whom he had loved were now trying to kill him.

No Sympathy

Ordinarily one would expect that God would come through with some kind of consoling message. One would think that God would have sympathized with Elijah. The least that God could have done would have been to applaud him and thank him for his faithfulness and that somehow God would reward him or pay him off at another time. Or maybe God could have said that every cloud has a silver lining and that some day Elijah would be able to see the fruits of his labors. God could have told Elijah that God would eventually set things right and make these people pay for their sins of unbelief.

You would think that at this point Elijah deserved some kind of pat on the head or gentle hand on the shoulder. No way! God offers no consoling word here. God does not weep one tear on behalf of Elijah. God appears to turn a deaf ear to the complaint. Instead, God says, "Go, return on your way to the wilderness of Damascus." God tells him to get back in there and pitch. Elijah is not to feel sorry for himself. He is to do what he is told to do. "Get on your way," says God. Get out of that cave of doubt that he had been hiding in. Move out from your hidden corner. Stop being cooped up in the cocoon of self and get with it. God refused to refuel the self-concern of Elijah and rudely awakened him to the fact that God still had work for him to do.

Setting the Agenda

God tells Elijah that he must get back on the job. He also set the agenda of work for Elijah. Elijah is to anoint Hazael to be king of Syria and Jehu to be king over Israel. In reality, Elijah did not have opportunity to anoint either of these men for their positions. It was Elisha, Elijah's successor, who eventually performed those rites. However, these acts appear to be inspired by Elijah, and there is no doubt but that Elijah passed on these instructions to Elisha. What should catch our attention, however, is the fact that it appears absolutely extraordinary that the prophet should be instructed to anoint Hazael as king over an enemy nation. Elisha did not actually anoint Hazael but informed him that he would be king. And Hazael, who was a servant to the king, murdered the king and took over his throne. Furthermore when Elisha did inform Hazael that he would be king of Syria he did so with tears in his eyes bemoaning the fact that Hazael would harrass both Israel and Judah, which Hazael did.

Jehu, on the other hand, did perform a function that would have pleased Elijah. He led an insurrection against the house of Ahab. Jehu had been a commander in the army of Israel. Elisha met him in camp and anointed him king, and the army in a coup acclaimed him king. He personally slew Joram,

Ahab's son and the present king, and had Joram's body thrown on the vineyard of Naboth in fulfillment of Elijah's prophecy. Jehu then returned to Jezreel where he ordered the servants of Jezebel to throw her down from the palace wall, and she was killed. Then Jehu had the entire family of Ahab destroyed. The result was that the worship of Baal was driven out from Israel.

Finding a Successor

God also informed Elijah that he should anoint the son of Shaphat, Elisha, as a prophet. Elisha, working with twelve sets of oxen and all the servants that would require, must have been from a wealthy home. We also surmise that he was very close to his family in that he requests permission to return to them for farewell kisses and adieus. Elisha also appears to be ready and willing to take on the role of prophet. He shows no hesitancy in giving up his life of affluence and comfort with his family. He speaks his goodbyes to friends and servants at a farewell feast that appears to have something of a sacrificial and sacramental character.

What is striking, however, is that Elisha is willing to step into the shoes of Elijah when everyone in Israel, the Northern Kingdom, had to know just how difficult things had been for him. Everyone knew that he was public enemy number one and that his life was on the line. Ahab had all the power of the throne working against Elijah at this point. Elisha was a ready servant of the Lord. Ordinarily a prophet was not anointed. Only kings and priests were. So once more the command to anoint the prophet is really a way of saying that the call should be extended to Elisha to carry on the work of Elijah.

God is In Charge

What all of this was to mean to Elijah is that life goes on.

But it meant far more than that. Life is not simply happenstance. God was not simply saying to Elijah, "chin up" and all that. He was not forcing Elijah to set his jaw and keep a stiff upper lip. That all may be courageous, but it can be silly, dangerous, and futile. In his instructions to Elijah God was saying that Elijah could get on with his work, because God was in charge. God knew what he was doing. God was in charge of the enemy, Hazael. God was in charge of his own people, Jehu. God was in charge of the faithful believer, Elisha. Through these people God had to work. God was content to deal with history through this people. God has no other way. God must work through the strengths as well as the weaknesses of people. God also has to accept the evil and the excesses of people. God has no pleasure in the radical behavior of anyone. But finally God's will is done in the world through it all.

What is even more important, Elijah could also take comfort in the fact that the destinies of the world are shaped by the prophetic creatures like Elijah and Elisha. What emerges from the careers of these two great prophets is that they were the ones who ultimately shaped the events in the world for the favor of God's people. For the people of God, life does not just go on. Life is in the hands of God and we can be sure that we are not just set adrift. We are in the world to go on our way serving and doing God's will as we know it in the power of God's Spirit. We can be brave, courageous and free in serving the purposes of God in whatever our vocations and callings may be.

The Bottom Line

The bottom line was also that God did give solid comfort to Elijah. God informed him that the leadership of Hazael, Jehu and the prophet Elisha would combine to work for the expulsion of Baal worship in Israel. Which it did. In addition, Elijah did not have to think he was the only faithful one left in Israel. There were seven thousand who had not yet bowed to Baal. Then when Elisha did follow after Elijah, we read "he arose and went after Elijah, and ministered to him." Elijah, who felt so alone, was not alone for a moment. God was with him all the way.

The lessons should be plain for us. No matter how deserted, how alone, and how paranoid we may feel about our position, we do not have to fear. What God demonstrated for Elijah through the likes of Hazael, Jehu and Elisha, God has perfected for us through our Lord Jesus Christ. On the Cross God demonstrated for us how God uses the forces of history to work out our salvation for us. Jesus was the King, the Priest, the Prophet, whom God himself anointed with the fulness of the Spirit to complete our salvation for us. All history gets rolled up into the life and death and resurrection of our Lord to assure us that we are never alone. So whenever we are feeling lonely or blue, God can say to us, "On your way with you. I'll be with you."

Now Naboth and Jezreelite had a vineyard in Jezreel, beside the palace of Ahab king of Samaria. And after this Ahab said to Naboth, "Give me your vineyard, that I may have it for a vegetable garden, because it is near my house; and I will give you a better vineyard for it; or, it if seems good to you, I will give you its value in money." But Naboth said to Ahab, "The Lord forbid that I should give you the inheritance of my fathers."

Then the word of the Lord came to Elijah the Tishbite, saying, "Arise, go down to meet Ahab king of Israel, who is in Samaria; behold, he is in the vineyard of Naboth, where he has gone to take possession. And you shall say to him, 'Thus says the Lord: "Have you killed, and also taken possession?"' And you shall say to him, 'Thus says the Lord: "In the place where dogs licked up the blood of Naboth shall dogs lick your own blood."'"

Ahab said to Elijah, "Have you found me, O my enemy?" He answered, "I have found you, because you have sold yourself to do what is evil in the sight of the Lord. Behold, I will bring evil upon you; I will utterly sweep you away, and will cut off from Ahab every male, bond or free, in Israel."

1 Kings 21:1-3, 17-21

1 Kings 21:1-3, 17-21   *Proper 9 (C)*
Pentecost 7 (L)
Ordinary Time 14 (RC)

One Word of Judgment

    Legislation in our country has made it difficult for some organizations and church groups to be critical of public policy and law. Churches and any tax-exempt organization can lose their tax-exempt status if they campaign against what is accepted public policy and law. A Christian magazine lost its tax-exempt status for a time, because it supported a candidate for president. A group of church officials was fined and threatened with losing their tax-exempt status because they opposed what was regarded as the "law of the land." The issue of intimidating the groups who might otherwise feel it their calling to serve as a conscience of the nation and community is a delicate one.
    On the one hand, we want to be sure that we do not disrupt a proper balance between church and state. On the other hand, our founding fathers never intended the doctrine of the separation of church and state to mean that the church should not influence the behavior of the state. That principle meant that the state should not establish any one church or faith as the established religion of the nation. However, the doctrine of the separation of church and state also recognizes the value that religion is to the welfare of the nation and how the government should also protect the rights and welfare of the churches. With that we need to recognize when the church can speak to or address issues in the nation.

A Case History

In the story of Elijah confronting King Ahab concerning Naboth's vineyard we have an ancient case history of how a prophetic figure confronted a top government official about ethical conduct. The situation was certainly one that Elijah must have loathed having to address. The story starts out simply enough. Naboth owned a vineyard that was a choice piece of property next to the palace of the king. The king thought it would be a good investment for him if he could annex the vineyard to his property to create a vegetable garden.

Ahab makes a fair and legitimate offer to Naboth. He was willing to make a trade for a larger vineyard, or he was willing to pay cash for whatever Naboth wanted to make his asking price. Naboth turned down the offer, and was within his rights in doing so. Naboth was not being stubborn, and the king could not claim eminent domain over this property. Naboth did not want to relinquish the inheritance of his fathers. The land belonged to Naboth through inheritance. The law protected such inheritance and was designed to encourage the families to keep the land they received by inheritance, so that the very precious and scarce property could be kept within the family and it could be worked properly by one generation after another.

Jezebel's Plot

Ahab recognized Naboth's right of refusal. However, he was greatly dejected, because he could not have what he so desperately wanted and slumped into some royal pouting. When Queen Jezebel discovered Ahab in this depressed state, she resorted to some of her usual cunning to devise a plot that would make it possible for King Ahab to take over the property in question. In the refusal Naboth had said to the King, "The Lord forbid that I should give you the inheritance of my fathers." Jezebel was not going to let anyone be so bold as to refuse the King. She sent off letters to the elders and nobles ordering them to set a trial for Naboth and to find two witnesses who would be willing to testify that Naboth had cursed God and the King. Naboth was charged with high crime in cursing the King and the sin of blasphemy in cursing God.

These were serious crimes in those primitive communities where people were fearful of invoking the anger of the gods, and people believed that kings ruled by divine right, that is, by the power from on high. The situation naturally would call for a public fast, because one had dared to risk the welfare of the community with such serious misdemeanors. Jezebel no sooner gave her orders, and the evil plot was consummated. None of the elders or nobles dared to protest this evil, and they all conformed to the Queen's wishes. Naboth was tried by this kangaroo court, was found guilty, and was taken out and stoned according to Hebrew law.

Enter Elijah the Prophet

No sooner had Naboth breathed his last than Jezebel urged her husband to go and take possession of the vineyard. Ahab responded to the news of Naboth's death by emerging from his deep depression and making tracks to the vineyard. He could hardly wait to get there. However, in the meantime there was action in another quarter. At the same time that Jezebel was dispatching her husband to the site of the vineyard, the Word of the Lord came to Elijah as to what was transpiring, and Elijah was prompted by that Word to intercept Ahab and confront him with the unethical manner in which Ahab was gaining possession of this property.

Elijah had completely recovered from his fear of the royal court. The prophet had been strengthened by the Word and the presence of Yahweh. After Elijah had returned from his spiritual retreat, he had been renewed by the Spirit of God and returned to the Northern Kingdom of Israel from which he had been banished. We have one account in which after he returned he had served as an advisor to the King and had counseled King Ahab in achieving significant victories over the archrival Assyrians. The significance of those victories was not to demonstrate that Elijah had gone soft on the King, or that he wanted to curry the favor of the King, but to give evidence once more that Yahweh was superior to the gods of the alien powers and that Yahweh could be trusted. Now Elijah would have to face Ahab for another reason.

The Confrontation

The confrontation in the vineyard was not a pleasant one. The occasion opened old wounds and created new ones. Ahab's joy at the prospect of taking over the vineyard quickly changed to gloom. "Have you found me O my enemy?", he asked Elijah. He knew that Elijah had not only located him but that the prophet had found him out. Elijah was direct and firm in the answer, "I have found you, because you have sold yourself to do what is evil in the sight of the Lord." Elijah went on to describe the kind of punishment that would befall Ahab. The royal house would be wiped out. The family would be literally destroyed by animals and Queen Jezebel, the Queen who was an imported princess from Phoenicia, would also be destroyed. What is so striking about this incident is the fact that from a political and administrative point of view Ahab had been an above-average ruler. He had made strong alliances, achieved military victories, engaged in the building of cities, encouraged some prosperity in the land, and brought some prestige to the people.

One innovation, inspired by Ahab's wife (whom he had married to strengthen a political alliance), was to import her deities into Israel so that the people would not have to go down to Jerusalem in the southern kingdom of Judah. While that had made for earlier confrontations between Ahab and the prophet Elijah, that did not spell his doom. Elijah uncovers the unethical behavior that exposes the royal couple for what they really were. One thinks of how this happens in our own time. A ruthless politico runs an administration with a mob, and goes untouched until government agents expose this person for income tax evasion. That has been repeated over and over again in the lives of high and low government officials who are nailed for income tax evasion, bribes, taking advantage of their positions for improper gains, or Watergate-style break-ins.

Where's the Gospel?

When we take a hard look at how quickly Elijah lowered the boom on Ahab, we ask ourselves, where is the Gospel in this story? Did the situation call for only a word of judgment? Could Elijah not have used some non-directive counseling to bring Ahab around? The truth of the matter is that God had demonstrated great patience with Ahab. God had given repeated evidences and signs of superiority over the foreign gods and demonstrated God's willingness to save this people God wanted to keep as a beloved people.

Ahab had refused the divine overtures that had been so dramatic, and Ahab's willingness to stoop to this cheap trick of destroying a little person like Naboth for the sake of a vegetable garden was the last straw. The lack of ethical discretion and the unjust execution of Naboth were symptoms of how perverted the rule of Ahab had become, because he refused God's gracious efforts to get to him. But Ahab did respond to the word of judgment. When he repented, God informed Elijah that God would postpone the destruction of Ahab's royal line for one whole generation.

A Model for Ministry

How Elijah applied the Word in the case of Ahab is an excellent model or paradigm to illustrate how we should minister with the Word today. Elijah brought a word of judgment, because that is all Ahab could respond to, if he were to respond at all. The good and gracious rule of God had been totally ignored by the ambitious royal couple previously. Ahab had to be convicted to the sin he had committed before he could repent. It is clear that his conscience had been troubled at the beginning of the meeting with Elijah in the vineyard. After he repented Ahab could contemplate the mercies and the grace of God and how necessary forgiveness and reconciliation were. People of the world today also experience the gracious activity of God in their lives in many ways. They may experience God's providence, goodness, strength and help over and over again without ever acknowledging their dependency upon God.

People may come to know how God demonstrated love for the world through our Lord Jesus Christ by seeing the way in which their neighbors believe and trust in the death and resurrection of Jesus Christ. They may come to know it by the universal witness to this Christ in the media, but they will know it more believably through the lives of their friends. However, they may be totally untouched by all of that. They may also be unmoved by the word of judgment that rides on the media's constant reporting of the danger of a nuclear holocaust. What they need is that personal word of judgment that exposes their unethical or immoral behavior. That Word clearly exposes the fact that they have not confessed their sins to God — or to their neighbors. Only then can they confess and receive absolution.

A Model for Attacking Public Sins

The story of Elijah and Ahab also gives us a pattern for the attacking of sins in high places. Many well-intentioned people sometimes confuse the Gospel of God's love in Jesus Christ with ethical behavior and the law. They would like to legislate the Gospel into law. Elijah could not do that. Nor could any of the prophets, nor our Lord himself. Nor should we expect that all those in high places will respond to the Gospel of love. When we work for justice in society, we do so through the law. Naboth sought his defense in the law. However, the law was perverted by his enemies.

Elijah used the law to expose the crime and also to pronounce judgment. In this instance Ahab apparently repented, and Ahab received some expression of grace for his repentance. However, the Law still brought the house of Ahab down within the next generation, because there was no further repentance. At the same time we have to know that the art of discerning when judgment is to fall on those in high places is not always easy, but must be pursued by all in society. When holy absolution is to be offered should not be all that difficult to determine. We should be able to see in the repentance of those who seek God's grace that they are just like us, sinners who daily need to come to God for grace.

Now when the Lord was about to take Elijah up to heaven by a whirlwind, Elijah and Elisha were on their way from Gilgal.

Then Elijah said to him, "Tarry here, I pray you; for the Lord has sent me to the Jordan." But he said, "As the Lord lives, and as you yourself live, I will not leave you." So the two of them went on. Fifty men of the sons of the prophets also went, and stood at some distance from them, as they both were standing by the Jordan. Then Elijah took his mantle, and rolled it up, and struck the water, and the water was parted to the one side and to the other, till the two of them could go over on dry ground.

When they had crossed, Elijah said to Elisha, "Ask what I shall do for you, before I am taken from you." And Elisha said, "I pray you, let me inherit a double share of your spirit." And he said, "You have asked a hard thing; yet, if you see me as I am being taken from you, it shall be so for you; but if you do not see me, it shall not be so." And as they still went on and talked, behold, a chariot of fire and horses of fire separated the two of them. And Elijah went up by a whirlwind into heaven. And Elisha saw it and cried, "My father, my father! the chariots of Israel and its horsemen!" And he saw him no more.

Then he took hold of his own clothes and rent them in two pieces. And he took up the mantle of Elijah that had fallen from him, and went back and stood on the bank of the Jordan. Then he took the mantle of Elijah that had fallen from him, and struck the water, saying, "Where is the Lord, the God of Elijah?" And when he had struck the water, the water was parted to the one side and to the other; and Elisha went over.

2 Kings 2:1, 6-14

2 Kings 2:1, 6-14

Proper 10 (C)
Pentecost 8 (L)
Ordinary Time 15 (RC)

One Vision of Glory

The story of the Transfiguration of our Lord evokes some mixed feelings. On the one hand, we can appreciate what this meant to Jesus. He knew that he was approaching the time of his arrest and crucifixion. The enemies were drawing the circle of animosity tighter. Jesus had experienced serious defections from his ranks. He needed to be strengthened for the ordeal ahead of him. For the intimate circle of disciples the Transfiguration was also meaningful. They had been following Jesus on the assumption that he was the Messiah. Yet they did not know how he would bring off his messianic coup. All their suggestions about the Kingdom thus far had been rejected by Jesus. Yet they persisted in their conviction that Jesus was the Messiah and they doggedly followed, in spite of the rebuffs they also received from the enemies of our Lord.

We can well imagine how thrilled the disciples were, then, to be privy to this glorious moment when our Lord is revealed in such obvious innocence and splendor. They could refer to this later as that moment when they beheld his glory and when they were given a more sure witness. (John 1:14 & 2 Peter 2:18) However, our question is, "How do we get in on the act?" We need assurances, too. When do we get a glimpse of the glory? That was the experience of Elisha who wanted to share in Elijah's moment of glory. That is the story of our Lesson appointed for the day, and we do well to see how we can identify with his experience.

The Prophet's Career

To understand this story we need to think back on the career of the prophet Elijah. He undoubtedly was one of the most outstanding persons in the succession of prophets. However, we do not have a collection of his writings, as we do from other great prophets. Furthermore, we note that his ministry was in the usually-faithless Northern Kingdom, not like most of the others who worked in Judah. However, we do have this marvelous collection of stories about his heroic and prophetic activity.

Elijah was a one-man resistance movement against the infamous King Ahab and his Queen Jezebel, that Phoenician beauty who had imported the system of baal worship from her native land. She had instituted the baal priesthood in Israel, a priesthood with whom Elijah waged serious conflict. One of the most dramatic stories in all of Scripture is the well-known account of how Elijah challenged the priests of Baal to a contest, with sacrifices first to their god and then to Yahweh, the God of Israel. Of course, you remember the outcome of that story. However, that is only one in a series in which Elijah outwitted and defeated the priests of Baal and the king himself. No other prophet accumulated such huge successes, and it was Elisha who prayed that he might follow in the steps of the prophet.

Elisha Follows

Elisha was "right on" about the importance of the ministry of Elijah. Certainly he could not have anticipated how Elijah was to be taken into heaven. That was not in the normal range of human experience. He *did* know that somehow God was going to translate Elijah into glory. One would naturally expect that to be by death. What he did know was that the era of Elijah was at an end. Yet he wanted the spirit of Elijah to continue in his ministry. So it was to be in the entire

Hebrew tradition. Elijah eventually was to be regarded as the most messianic-like figure. The messianic hope was built on the notion that the Messiah would come when Elijah returned. To this day, every Seder meal is celebrated with a vacant chair reserved for the returning Elijah.

One can appreciate, then, Elisha's persistance in following Elijah. It is akin to the attitude of the disciples in following Jesus. Beyond that, we ought also to appreciate the fact that Elisha was not following out of some form of desperation, or because he had nothing else to do. When Elisha was first called by Elijah, he had been plowing with twelve yoke of oxen, an indication that he was a person of considerable wealth. Elisha was willing to forsake all in order to follow Elijah. He sacrificed his oxen to the Lord to celebrate the occasion. It was also typical of Elisha that, from the day he started to follow Elijah to the end of his prophetic career, he demonstrated intense energy and exemplary faithfulness.

Elijah's Reluctance

However, as we read this story of the Translation of Elijah, we are puzzled by the reluctance of Elijah to permit Elisha to accompany him to the exciting conclusion of his ministry. Elijah tells Elisha to wait at Gilgal, because the Lord was sending him to Bethel. Elisha protests and says that nothing can prevent him from remaining with Elijah. A school of prophets at Bethel also come out to discourage Elisha, because they sense that God is going to take Elijah from him. Elisha acknowledges their premonition but ignores their advice. He continues on to Bethel, that shrine of the Northern Kingdom, that had also been plagued with baalism.

Once more, Elijah requests that Elisha stay there while he answers the Lord's summons to go to Jericho, that infamous city that had first fallen to the Hebrews when they entered the Promised Land. Once more, Elisha pledges his allegiance, and again prophets from that city come to warn Elisha of Elijah's imminent departure. He is undaunted by their warning. A third time Elijah orders Elisha to stay, because he has been sent by God to the Jordan. Elisha offers his protest once more. When Elijah parts the waters of the Jordan as Joshua had done before him and Moses had done at the Red Sea, Elisha ignores the stares of the prophets who are watching and continues with Elijah to the other side. Elisha is a person who is not to be denied. His faithfulness is not a blind following but rather a confidence that he can and will be blessed by Elijah.

Elisha's Persistance

Elisha ignored the advice of the schools of the prophets at three different junctures. Whether they were putting him down or putting him off made no difference. Perhaps they were saying to him that life would never be the same without Elijah. Maybe it was professional jealousy. It could be that they thought their own roles as prophets would be greatly enhanced when Elijah was gone. Or they may have been suggesting to Elisha that he could never match the manner in which Elijah had worked and achieved such high distinction. This could have been their way of eliminating the competition. Whatever they were trying to lay on Elisha made no impact on him whatsoever. He followed on. They may have been Elisha's tempters, but he would not be tempted.

From the other side, the tests came from Elijah. One would or could expect that the mentor Elijah would have been flattered by the way in which his chief disciple followed him so closely. Yet it is Elijah who also discourages Elisha. Three times he mentions that God has a special assignment for him, but he does not include Elisha in the mandate. Yet each time he capitulates to Elisha and takes him along. Each time Elisha is more deeply entrenched in his conviction that he belongs at the side of this spiritual leader. Each time he participates in the prophetic assignments in a deeper commitment to what it is that God expects of his servants. It is an emotional scene each time, to be sure. However, it is also deeply spiritual. Elisha is not poking along to share in the glory, or because he is sentimental about his relationship with Elijah. Elisha is there because he is a prophet and he wants to be a better prophet.

A Brilliant Request

Elijah understands the motives of Elisha. After Elijah performs that ultimate sign of the prophetic office that identified him with Moses and Joshua, the parting of the Jordan, he turns to Elisha and says, "Ask what I shall do for you, before I am taken from you." Elisha answered, "I pray you, let me inherit a double share of your spirit." That did not mean that Elisha wanted to have twice as much authority or power for his prophetic office as Elijah had. That is a bothersome petition. We may think this would be dreadfully egotistical of Elisha, and we may wonder why God would give in to such an outlandish request.

What the request meant was that, like the law assigned to the first-born son, Elisha asked for two portions of the prophetic spirit as an inheritance from his spiritual father. That was a thoughtful and proper request. Elijah answered that this was a hard thing. If, however, Elisha did see when Elijah was being taken from him, the prayer would be granted. If he did not see, the prayer would be denied. That, of course, was the final obstacle placed before Elisha. If Elijah thought this request of Elisha's was difficult, then certainly Elisha would respond that this was also difficult. The other impediments that had been placed before him appeared to be much more manageable, since this one would seem to be dealing with the unknown.

The Event

As Elijah and Elisha went on their way talking, a chariot of fire and horses of fire separated the two of them, and Elijah went up into heaven in a whirlwind. Who is there to explain this spectacular phenomenon? We have only the memory of it through the one who witnessed it, Elisha. Yet we know this singular experience was so deeply imbedded in the soul of the Hebrew people that they were confident that Elijah would be the messianic figure or the precursor of the Messiah. So it was that, when our Lord came, some thought that he was *Elijah redivivus*, Elijah revived. Or some thought that John the baptizer was Elijah returned. Both denied that. Yet the evangelist could report that when our Lord was on the Mount of the Transfiguration that Moses was there. And all of us can be sure that the Translation of Elijah into heaven prefigured that day when we are to be translated into heaven, and that great day when our dear Lord returns to gather us into his Kingdom.

All that aside, for the moment we cannot forget what this meant to Elisha. When this happens in that flashing and fiery moment, Elisha saw it. He *saw* it. He saw it. And he cried, "My father, my father. The chariots of Israel and its horsemen!" And then he saw him no more. It was all over. The Translation of Elijah was all over. But it was not over for Elisha. He had seen, and his prayer was granted. He launched on a prophetic career filled with bravery and prophetic boldness and signs that almost matched that career of Elijah he worked so hard to emulate. When Elijah entered into glory (that is, the presence of God) Elisha drew from the experience in order to work his ministry.

Your Vision

Now you can understand how you get the vision of the glory at the Mount of Transfiguration or the glory of the Translation of Elijah at the Jordan. The vision of the glory is *faith*. Elisha saw what God had done for Elijah, *because he had the faith to see*. In faith Elisha answered the call to follow Elijah in the beginning. Faith kept Elisha in the train of Elijah all the way until he saw Elijah in the whirlwind. We enter the

Mount of Transfiguration by the same route. We see our Lord revealed as the Son of God. By the spirit of faith we know what Jesus did for us. We know he died and rose again for us. We know he redeemed us from sin. We know he conquered hell for us. We know that he is present always in our lives through temptation and trial.

To know all that is to have the vision. It is *to see*. It is to know to see what the world cannot see. It is to know that God is ruling in all things. It is to know that God will sustain us. It is to know that we can be blessed with the powers from on high even as Elisha was. To have the vision is to persist, like Elisha, when we pray that God would grant us a proper share of our inheritance of the prophetic.

God wants us to see. He is not playing games with us. Faith will help you to see that he is always with you and for you. To see that is to be covered with glory.

About the Author

Harry N. Huxhold, a native of Forest Park, Illinois, a modest western suburb of Chicago, attended preparatory school in Milwaukee, Wisconsin. He holds the M.Div. degree from Concordia Theological Seminary, St. Louis; the M.Th. from Luther Northwestern Theological Seminary, St. Paul; and the D.Min. (cum laude) from Christian Theological Seminary, Indianapolis. He also did graduate studies in social and industrial relations at Loyola, Chicago.

Pastor Huxhold has spent most of his ministry in the parish, having served a rural parish in Wisconsin, a suburban parish southwest of Chicago, and for over twenty years in a central city parish in Indianapolis. He has served as an executive in the welfare ministry of the church and also as a teacher. He was a campus pastor at the University of Minnesota for five years, and at different intervals taught while still serving as parish pastor. He taught religion in a Lutheran high school in Chicago and at Valparaiso University. He also taught homiletics and supervised students on the seminary level in Indianapolis.

Ecumenically, Pastor Huxhold has served as an assistant bishop in his denomination, served on a task force in the creation of the Evangelical Lutheran Church of America, was a part of the dialogue team in the national Methodist — Lutheran Dialogue, and is president of the Church Federation of Greater Indianapolis. He helped to found an ecumenical church council to serve the central city, and he is also president of his church's child and family services agency in Indianapolis.

As an auther Huxhold has contributed some forty articles to theological journals and religious periodicals. In addition he has had published fifteen books of devotional and sermonic materials.

www.ingramcontent.com/pod-product-compliance
Lightning Source LLC
Chambersburg PA
CBHW060851050426
42453CB00008B/940